On The Downs
and other *illustrated* poems

John Tatum

Cover artwork © John Tatum 2019

Book and cover design © FayJay 2019

Copyright © John Tatum 2019

On The Downs
and other *illustrated* poems

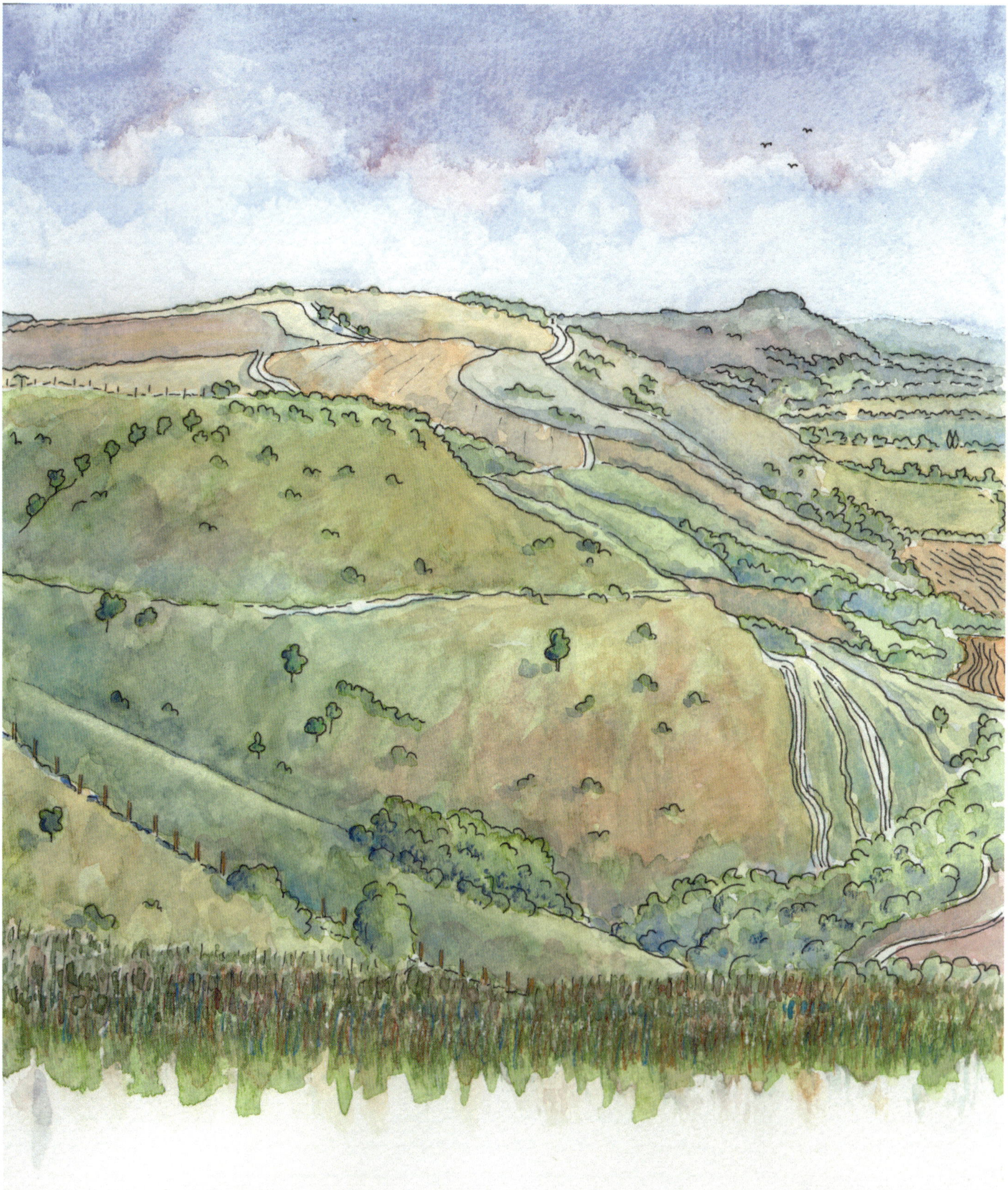

This book is dedicated to my wife, Greta, author of 'Lost Voices and Other Stories'.

Contents

ON THE DOWNS	1
THE BROADWOOD MORRIS MEN ON MAY DAY EVE	2
CRICKET MATCH	3
SUNDAY MORNING IN THE RAIN	5
CASTLE RUINS	6
BEACHCOMBING	7
SUSSEX STAG NIGHT	9
EVENING AT THE WHITE HORSE	10
THE REINCARNATE	11
OLD PEOPLE'S WARD	12
HARVEST THANKSGIVING	13
OLD BOB	14
RAIN, AT LAST	15
THE TITFIELD THUNDERBOLT	16
JACK AND NANCY'S WEDDING	17
THE PATH ON THE DOWNS	18
THE STATUE IN THE GARDEN	19
CATHEDRAL BUILDERS	21
THE DROWNED CATHEDRAL	22
THE GHOST	23
WAYFARERS' DOLE	24
BLADDERWRACK	27
WAITING FOR THE FIDDLER	28
THE SUN	29
EVERYTHING'S AS IT SHOULD BE IN THE WORLD	30
OF MORRIS DANCERS	31

ON THE DOWNS

Always, somehow, on these truly perfect days,
A bumblebee will be about her business
For hours and hours along her secretly chartered ways,
Giving definition to an almost endless stillness.
And, in that stillness, is a lark somewhere;
And distant farm sounds drifting on the air

But these perfect times are never still -
Passing like cloud shadows on the fields below
That dissolve so swiftly on that distant hill,
Seeming to leave us nothing as we turn to go.
But then, half heard, a distant church bell rings
And, from a nearby bush, an evening blackbird sings.

THE BROADWOOD MORRIS MEN ON MAY DAY EVE

From the Scarlett Arms in Wallis Wood they went,
On what to some would seem a crazy lark;
A crowd of eccentric Englishmen, but lent
The spirit of their forebears in the dark.

And so on Leith Hill beneath the stars,
By the tower that stood so black against the sky,
They danced and played away the midnight hours
To affirm anew that life would never die.

The reeling legs of the accordionist
Took him back and forth across the sward,
But not a single note his fingers missed;
And, *Dance, you merry men!* he roared.

On and on they danced and round them spun
The sky, the stars, the black shapes of the trees.
And it was as if the world had just begun,
The first corn stirring in the first breeze.

And then, with the music stopped; the dancers gone
Off down the hill and through the woods to home,
In the sudden hush and stillness May was born
And the Earth breathed all around with life re-sown.

CRICKET MATCH

Three grizzled greybeards on a bench -
Old Harry, Tom and Ned -
Through drowsy eyes each watch the game
And nods each aged head,

Hearing the sounds of earlier games
Come wafting on the breeze;
While the willow wings the leather high
Above the aged trees.

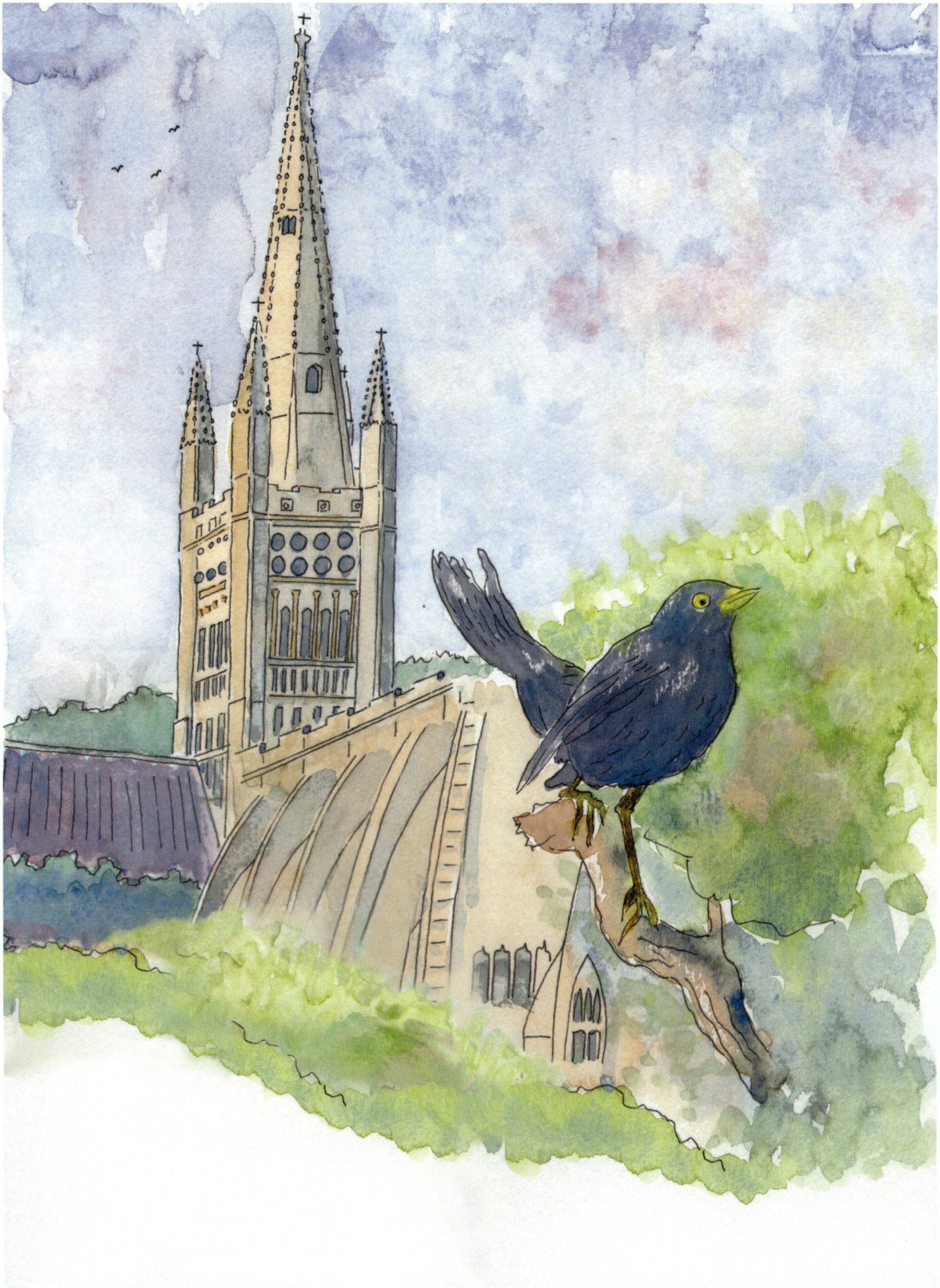

SUNDAY MORNING IN THE RAIN

A shaft of liquid, golden dawn
Breaks through the darkness of a storm.

Cathedral bells bring Heaven down
Across the rooftops of the town,

Buffeting a myriad sleeping heads,
Shuddering the timbers of their beds.

Gargoyles grimace through the rain
Each time the bells ring out again.

And through rain's hiss and bells' ding-dong
A blackbird sings his morning song.

CASTLE RUINS

Through the courts of history
Pale ghosts come and go,
Shivering the ivy on the walls
As they pass to and fro.

Their distant laughter
Drifts across the dawn
And shafts of sunlight
Quiver on the lawn.

Where no trees are, shadows play
Across the smooth-shorn grass,
Under an azure sky
Where no clouds pass.

BEACHCOMBING

We never know from day to day
What comes in on the tide –
Some relic of a lifelong gone
The ocean's tried to hide.

A piece of driftwood, green and smooth;
A bottle from afar,
Bobbing on the shining surf
And gleaming like a star.

Flotsam of history, love and war,
At one with stone and shell;
Words worn smooth and echoes of
Some long-since silenced bell.

We always live in hope, my love;
We know not what's in store.
So come with me and let us search
For sovereigns on the shore.

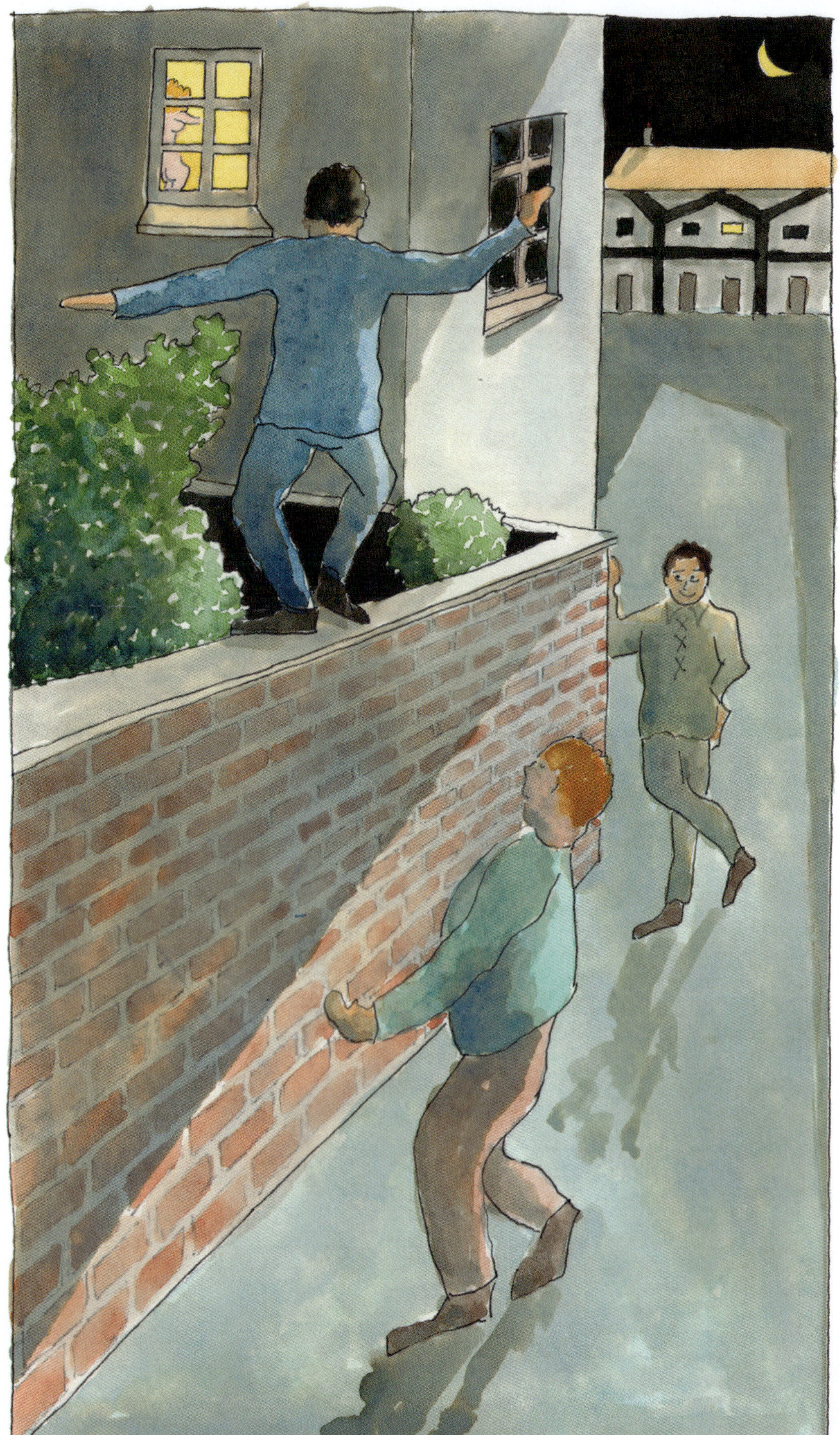

SUSSEX STAG NIGHT

The moon goes reeling through the trees
And Jack's atop the vicar's garden wall.
The steeple leans against the scudding clouds
And Jack looks like about to fall.
And it's hush, hush, my Sussex bonny boys,
Go home quiet and make no noise!

Young Nancy's shadow moves across the curtain.
We love her, lads, and that's for true.
Climb up, young Jack, upon this branch,
And then you'll get a better view!
And it's hush, hush, my Sussex bonny boys,
Go home quiet and make no noise!

Strike up on your harmonica, young Jack,
And we'll do a proper Morris dance.
Oh dear, he's in the flower bed now.
Get up, Jack, and let us see you prance.
And it's hush, hush, my Sussex bonny boys,
Go home quiet and make no noise!

It's all right, Officer, we've only drunk a yard of ale;
Though I swear young Jack drank from a pail.
And it's hush, hush, my Sussex bonny boys,
Go home quiet and make no noise!
Hush, hush, the clock's tolled midnight now.
Go home, lads, and make no noise.

EVENING AT THE WHITE HORSE

From the games room
Comes a clash of skittles,
Soft thud of darts,
Click of ancient ha'pennies;

The clatter and clash
Of Toad-in-the-Hole -
While through the hatch flow endlessly
Tankards of old ale.

A bull's-eye 's missed; the champion
Loves the landlord's daughter
Someone plays a squeezebox
And, behind the songs and laughter,

In the waiting dark
Beech leaves rustle;
A vixen barks, the blackbird
Gives a final whistle.

THE REINCARNATE

That landscape which bred me
Flickers before me. I can see,
From many a different viewpoint,
Superimposed faint
Images of the Downs;
Of small, half-timbered towns;
Of the stream which has meandered
Half-a-league since I wandered
Along its banks. They have cut
Down half the woodland. The spot
Where I lay is under wheat.
The path where your light feet
Trod is hidden by thorn;
Drowned is the place where I was born.

For centuries I was ivy,
Dog-rose, coarse grass. Perhaps happy
I was; but now am baked in bread
And brewed in ale and can enjoy instead
A song or two; entrance
A worthy fellow to get up and dance.

Soon, high above the world, I'll soar
On sweet currents of the air.

OLD PEOPLE'S WARD

She won't go back home now. Things are such
They'll never let her die *there*.
She'll never see again the spindly walnut table,
The miniatures grouped halfway up the stair.

She'll never see her chintzy curtains, stirring
In a summer breeze; nor hear again
The chiming of her ancient clock -
Although she *feels* them, far beyond her pain.

But, now - through her tiny leaded windows
(Beyond her bed the doctor frowns),
She sees all the seasons' skies;
Hears a blackbird, sees a small fold of the Downs.

HARVEST THANKSGIVING

Pigeons flap from spire to buttress,
Golden sunlight catching on their wings.
And, chortling as if he would outdo the bells,
A blackbird in the bishop's garden sings.

Beyond the city walls, rooks and seagulls
Find circles of companionship above the fields.
And, above the chugging of his ancient engine,
The tractor-driver hears the distant peals.

Then, suddenly, from half-a-dozen villages,
Clangs counterpoint from stubby Saxon towers.
Through city streets, down country lanes folk come
With baskets full of fruit and flowers.

OLD BOB

No, you can't come and drill here!
Shouted Old Bob, brandishing a broom
From the doorway of his chicken shed
And the oilman couldn't believe his ears.
You can't come and drill here!

You'd make a fortune if we struck oil!
Said the oilman, eyeing the rusty plough
Half-hidden in a nettle bed.
That's as maybe, answered Old Bob,
But you can't come and drill here!

He lurched across the muddy yard,
Squawking chickens scattering as he went.
I'll tell you once and for all, he said,
Waving his arms in his scarecrow coat,
You can't come and drill here!

A cockerel strutted on the broken gate,
His feathers ruffled by the wind
That tousled the old man's silvery head
And sent the sycamores waving wildly.
You can't come and drill here!

The Land Rover bumped back down the lane,
bruising the hedge. *Don't ever come back!*
My sons will take over after I'm dead!
Yelled tiny Bob in the rear-view mirror.
You can't come and drill here!

RAIN, AT LAST

We had never welcomed it in years before.
Always grumbled, but made it the subject
Of endless conversation - yet thought it a bore.

But now strangers smile at each other
To see it dampening the dusty streets
And, in spite of summer clothes, don't run for shelter

They let the crystal droplets fall about their heads,
Breathe deep the tang of freshened air
And give up worrying about their flower beds.

The strange clouds pile high above the town
In fantastic shapes shot through with gold
While, like a benediction, the rain pours down.

Others, in the distance, hang above the Weald
Where lost, sweet smells rise from the earth
And grasses nod, long last, in every tired field.

THE TITFIELD THUNDERBOLT

trundles between wooded hills,
shuffling little clouds of steam
into the fragrant summer air
of an age that might have been.

The ministry man's on board
Dan 's requisitioned home.
The countryside goes jerking by,
the wheels creak and groan.

The bishop shovels coals,
the vicar taps the glass.
It must be in God's hands
whether they fail or pass.

She puffs and chugs up gradients;
then hoots and hoots again,
as she races down the long slope
towards the water crane.

JACK AND NANCY'S WEDDING
(from Jack Clout the Ringer)

Rooks hang over distant stubble fields
In gaps in ranks of yew.
Across jig-saw shapes between the elms
Drift clouds in infinite blue.

The bells clang out merrily
As the lovers blink into the sun,
Jack and Nancy holding hands
And joined forever as one.

The vicar bobs upon his porch,
Smiling at ploughman and squire.
And behind never-dreamt-of relations
Follows the laughing choir

Now as Jack and Nancy walk in love
And pass through the old lychgate,
They little know that, in these lines,
Eternal life is their fate.

THE PATH ON THE DOWNS

The path slips sideways; clods
rumble down the slope.
Perhaps it's time to stop awhile,
take stock; though what I hope
to find might end in tears:
a contemplation of those wasted years.

It seems all paths, like this,
have led to nowhere,
except to dreams that could not last.
Now I can only stand and stare
out across the world below,
as if distance could reclaim the past.

THE STATUE IN THE GARDEN

Ah, you stone goddess,
at once so aged and young,
were your lips once mortal flesh
that smiled and sweetly sung?

The endless years pass swiftly by,
with all their pleasure and pain;
yet here you stand, serene and wise,
wearing away in the rain.

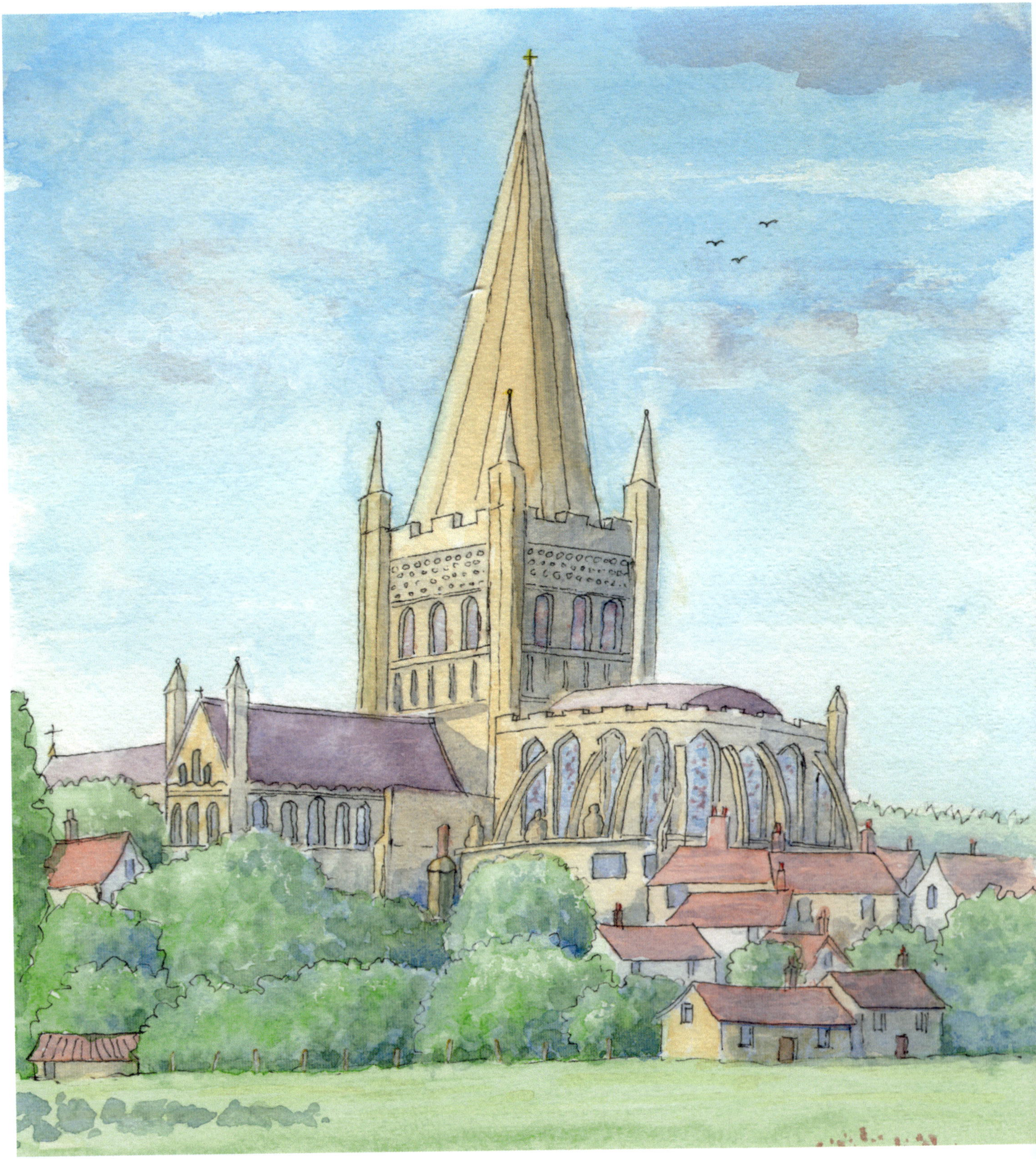

CATHEDRAL BUILDERS

We erect our wooden scaffolding
in Sussex, Kent and Devon.
We heave our blocks of stone to raise
our monuments to Heaven.

Bullock carts crawl like beetles
over the rim of the Earth,
bringing merchandise to sell
for far more than *we're* worth.

We see the townsfolk beneath us
haggling over their grain;
or, like so many ants in alleyways,
scurrying out of the rain.

They creep through the aisles like termites,
as they come to mouth their prayers;
or to gape at us as if we were
a troupe of performing bears.

The cathedral is *our* creation;
our muscles crack and bleed.
But the priests swig the sacramental wine
and pay us no heed.

High under hail's scourge or sun's glare,
we are close to God, we know.
Even when the wind tries to topple us
into the streets below.

THE DROWNED CATHEDRAL

Do you remember where the ivy climbed the crumbling wall?
    Yes, yes, I remember it well.
And where the ancient yew tree grew so tall?
    Yes, of course, before it fell.
That was where the bishop took his constitutional.
    Yes, yes, I remember it well.

They say a ghost tap-tapped among the graves.
    Ah yes, in those far-off, half-forgotten days.

And do you recall the sound of the solitary bell?
    Yes, yes, I remember that well.
And the tower where near the end it tolled the knell?
    Yes, of course, I remember it well.
They say the devil himself came up from hell.
    Yes, yes, they so do tell.

Everything's long gone now beneath the waves.
    Ah yes, even the poor old ghost with his friendly ways.

THE GHOST

At dawn of day by the castle she walks,
a lady dressed in white,
with silks and hair by zephyrs toyed
and hands clasped tight.

The dew-damp grass bears no print
and, as the morning light
flashes between the crumbling walls,
she vanishes from sight.

WAYFARERS' DOLE

"Please can you give me the Wayfarers' Dole, Sir?"
ventured the old gentleman of the road,
at the almshouse of St. Cross by Winchester town,
and the hand came through the porter's hatch
with the hunk of bread and the drinking horn.

    He thanked God as he drank his fill
    then tottered across the tussocky grass
    back to the ditch where his bundle lay
    and rummaged for an old striped scarf
    he'd got from a lady down Portsmouth way

"I'd like for to have that Wayfarers' Dole!"
he cried, stooped in his scarf and a mildewed hat,
risking a friendly wink and a crafty leer;
and the horn of plenty appeared again,
filled to the brim with golden beer

    He stumbled back once more to the ditch
    and, crouching under the windy sky,
    exchanged his jerkin for an old great coat.
    He tugged at elastic tangled in his rags;
    out sprang an eye-patch, a last convincing note.

"Gimme the Wayfarers' Dole, my friend!"
he bellowed, and he grabbed the horn,
slopping some beer on the hallowed ground.
The sunlight spun in the naked trees
and the bells of St. Cross rang all around.

    As sunlight chased shadows over the fields,
    he pulled on a cap from his friend who'd died.
    Then he sat in his ditch and laughed out loud,
    and with an old knife he hacked at his beard.
    He was a young man now and tall and proud.

"I demand my Wayfarers' Dole!" he boomed;
and out again came the hand through the hatch,
as it had for seven-hundred years or more.
The road lay white and distant hills swam near;
birds sung in the trees where none had before.

    He lay in his ditch on a bed of dead leaves
    and smiled at the flying clouds; his disguises
    strewn around, the horn empty at his side.
    He knew then all he'd never known
    in the last few moments before he died.

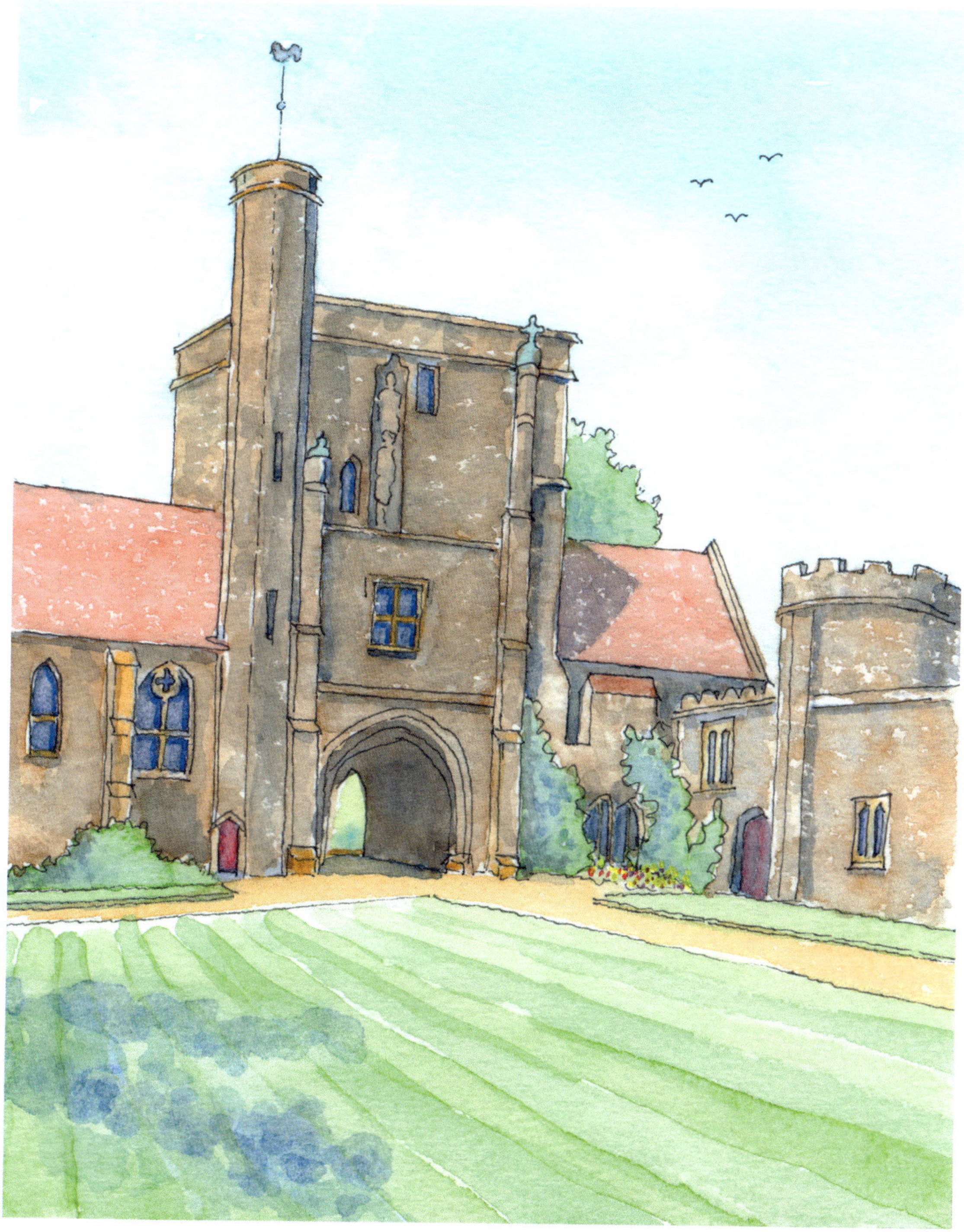

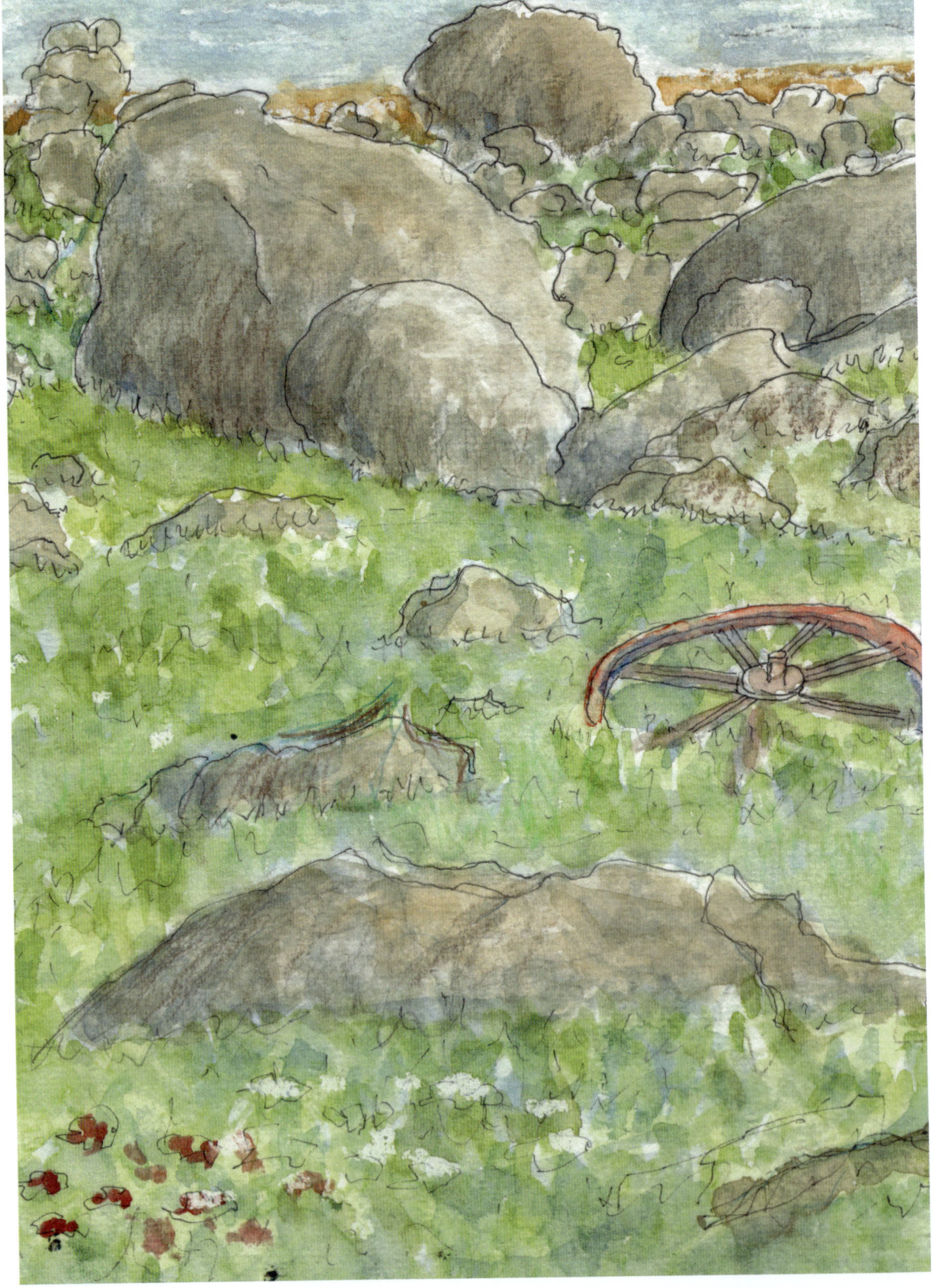

BLADDERWRACK
(for Dawn and Tony)

While sorting through old papers,
receipts, letters, an unpaid fine,
I found a sketch I'd long forgotten:
Skye, circa 1960. A stretch of ragged coastline.

I'd half a mind to screw it up
(the ball point, the yellowing lined paper)
but something stayed my hand -
a life long-gone perhaps. But what was actually *there*?

Gatherings of pebbles between boulders,
landward rocks half-sunk in turf;
a broken cartwheel lost in long grasses;
the slow dialogue of rain and surf.

I felt again the discomfort where I'd sat,
searching for my pen amid the stones;
and felt the sense of oblivion, strangely welcome,
as dampness seeped into my bones.

Has it stayed the same there, under that
low sky, through the long years' passing;
no dredger on the horizon, no
drinks cans, no plastic, no oiled wing;

only a piece of bladderwrack
snagged between rocks, the distant crashing
of waves and shingle's roar; the wind
in the ears of my ghost and seabirds crying?

WAITING FOR THE FIDDLER

Beams sag; the windowsill
has settled into history;
drink confirms the floorboards
point towards infinity.

A grandfather clock's
my sole companion here;
the ancient pub chair creaks
as I lean to sup my beer.

I see through bottle-glass
a field against a drizzly sky
and, like errant punctuation marks,
a bird or two drifts by.

At last! A figure with a fiddle case
hurries down the hill; small
yet as a beetle. And there's his photo,
thumb-tacked on the wall.

A door bangs - boots and voices
jostle in the corridor;
as I rise for a hurried refill
my chair-leg scrapes the floor.

The bar-maid's ready waiting then,
all friendly, pert and plump
and soon another pint of ale
comes gushing from the pump.

Suddenly the place is full
and I'm a stranger there;
but soon the music fills the room,
a haunting violent air.

No stranger then am I,
amid that gleeful throng.
I sup my ale and stamp my feet
and know that I belong.

THE SUN

I walked alone. The day was dark.
I wandered slowly through the park
Until I came into a wood
And there, transfixed, I stopped and stood.
For there I saw the old king, Sun,
Shining his armour with his thumb
And when the gold had lost its stain
He fell to rubbing it again.
"I think it better to be sure,"
He cried, and rubbed it more and more.
But soon he rose with agile prance
And did a most delightful dance.
"Forgive me for my sorry state,
Forgive me for my being so late;
I'm never usually so long
Getting my golden armour shone,
But I was in a lover's swoon
Trying to woo my mistress, Moon."
He let out then a joyous shout
As he whirled madly round about.
"But now it's done, my armour's done!"
Cried merrily the old king, Sun.

EVERYTHING'S AS IT SHOULD BE IN THE WORLD

Our worthy vicar's running up to bowl
and God the Father's smiling on his soul.

A doughty blacksmith strikes the ball
and who, but God, can say where it will fall?

Up the leather goes into the blue.
The crowd falls silent, the cows they cease to moo.

Like a meteor then the ball descends and lands
plumb straight into our reverend's waiting hands.

The next man in, a schoolboy full of hope,
soon goes off quickly looking like a dope.

Next a ploughboy, next the squire -
but our worthy vicar never seems to tire.

The captain of the visitors gives a sigh
as yet again the stumps are smashed awry.

And it will be recalled for ever more
how the challengers were all out for fifty-four.

A blackbird chortles loudly from an orchard bough
and a robin answers shrilly from a rusty plough.

Everything's as it should be, thank the Lord
us lads are playing cricket on the sward;

and the girls are where they were ordained to be:
in the pavilion making sandwiches and tea.

OF MORRIS DANCERS

Up and down they go. Up and down
beneath the great beech tree.
Of the loam they were born
and dance as merry as can be
until to the loam they will return.

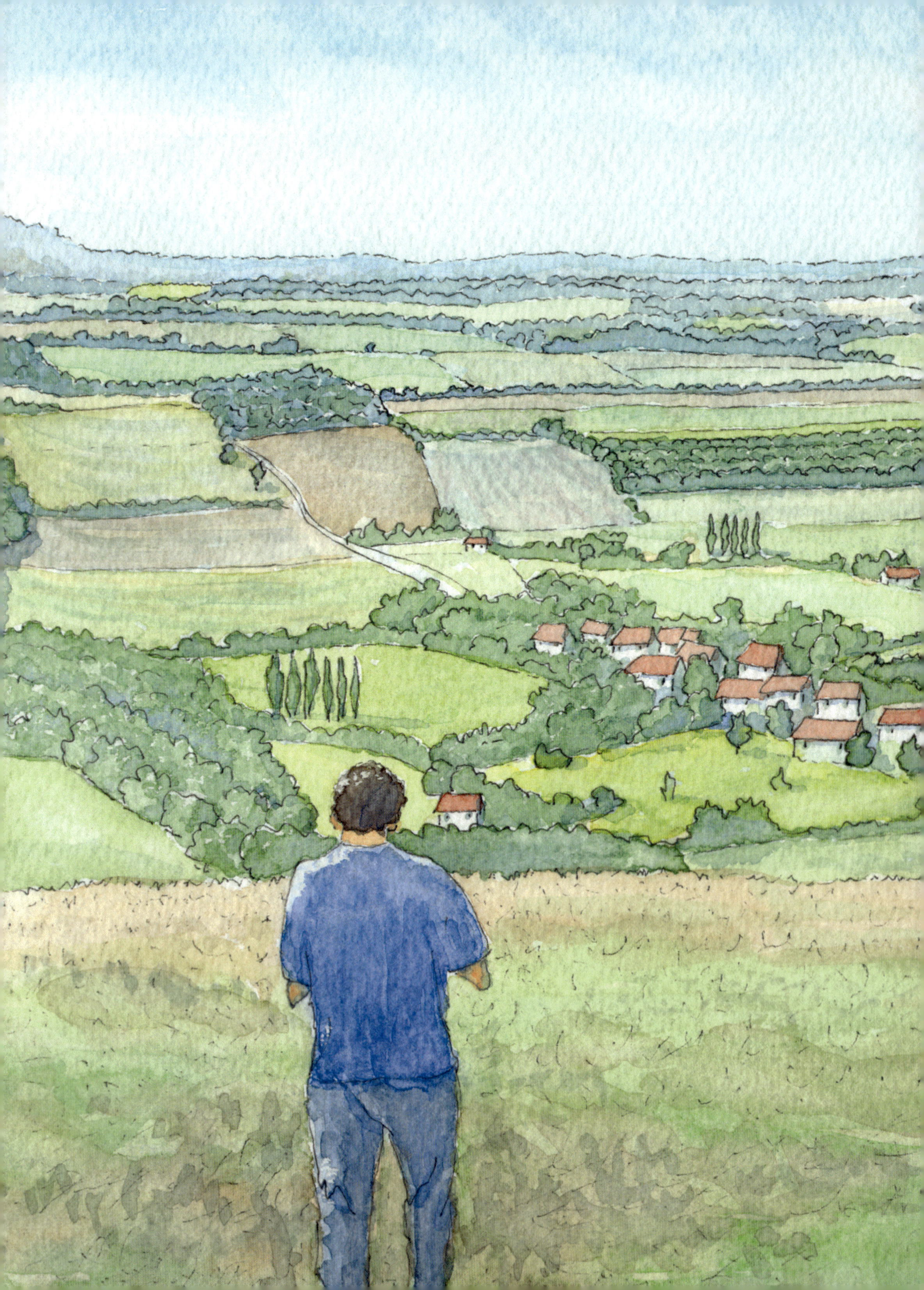

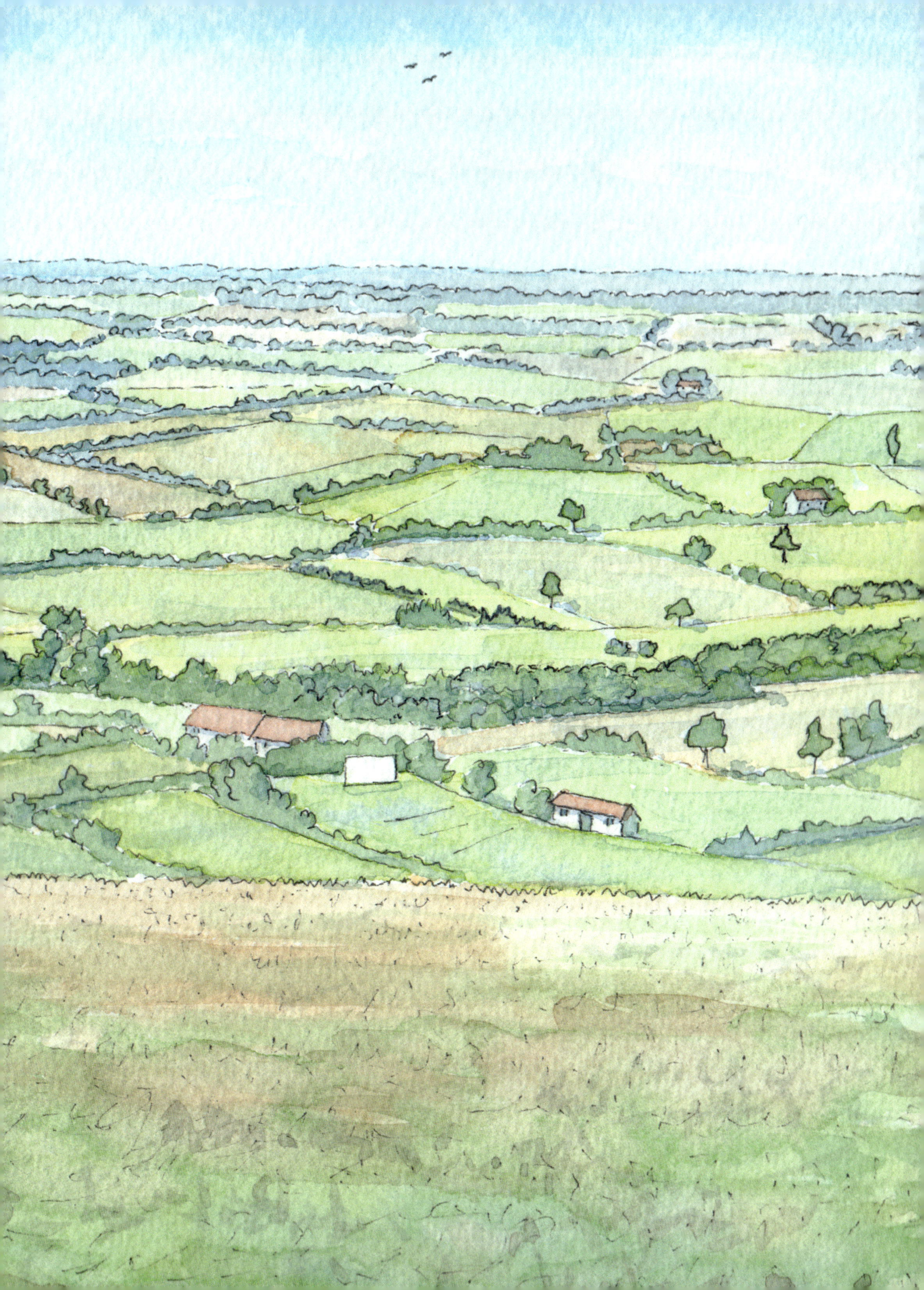

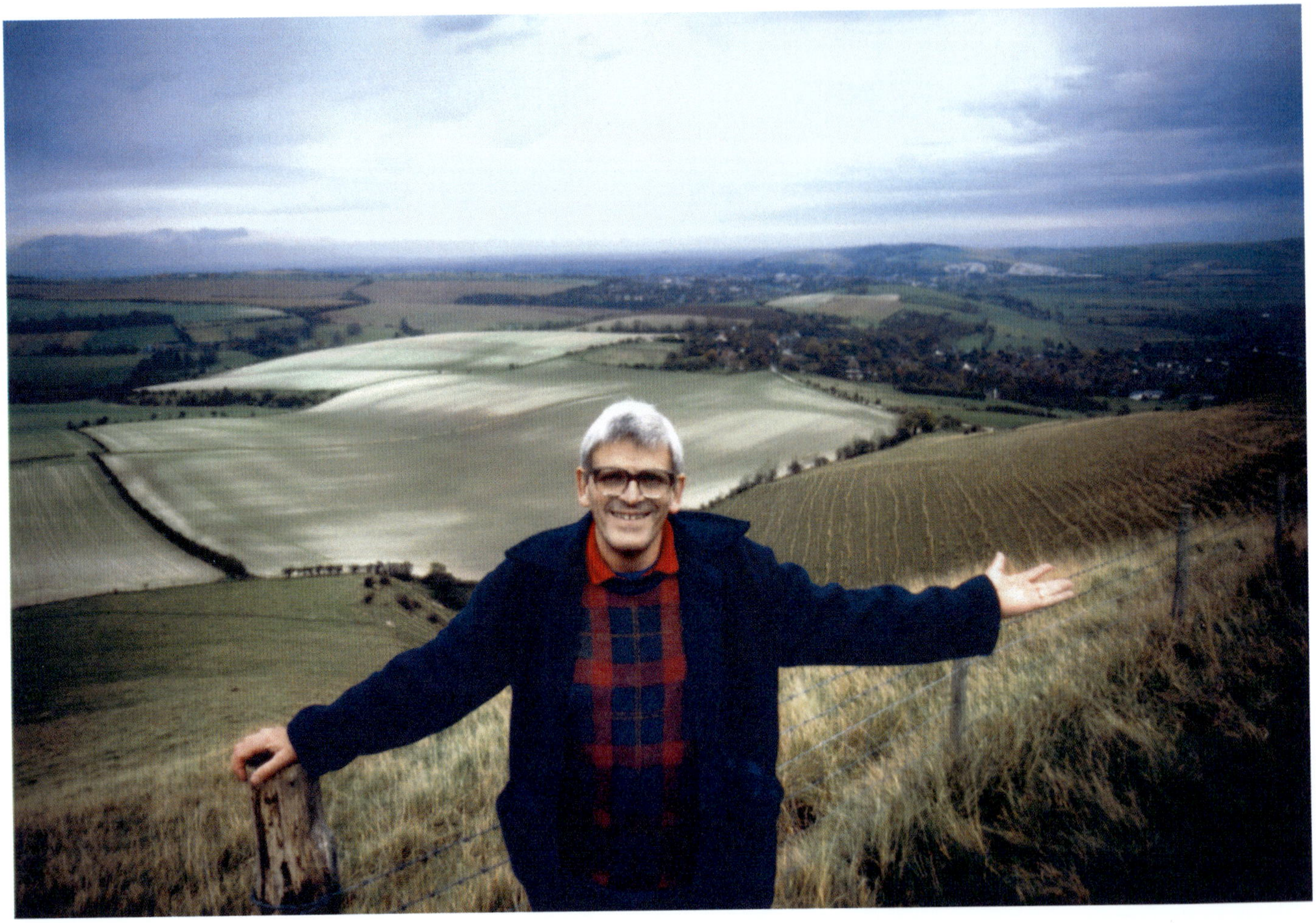

John Wyndham Tatum was born in Edinburgh in 1933 and educated at Shebbear College in Devon, where he was taught an appreciation of painting and poetry by Jackson Page.

'A View of the Town' (Outposts) was published in 1960 when he also became a member of 'The Group'. 'Poems to Sunday Notes of Jazz', on which he also played trumpet, was broadcast on BBC Radio 3 as part of Charles Fox's 'Jazz in Britain' series.

In 1984 he gained an Art Certificate at Brighton Art College where he was taught to draw and paint by Faith O' Reilly. He attended Ruskin College, Oxford, in 1997 to further develop his poetry.

He is the author of two volumes of collected poems, 1948-2018, under the titles of 'Towards an Unknown Fiction' and 'An Explosion of Skittles', funded by Arts Council England and published by Waterloo Press. He is also the author of two unpublished novels; 'Professor Meredith's Magic Universe' and 'The Stagglesford Chronicles'.

Life's circumstances have placed John Tatum in towns but he has always felt himself to be a countryman at heart.

"In the last verse of Everything's as it Should be in the World' I was being mischievous—it is not what I believe!"

Acknowledgements are due to This England, Evergreen, About Larkin, Reach, Envoi, Lookout, Yellow Crane, Robert Bloomfield Anthology, West Sussex Gazette, Argus, Wendy Webb books.

Printed in Great Britain
by Amazon